Ho\

MW01227088

DEDICATION

I dedicate this book to the woman who started it all, Eula Lee Fuller
– my Grandmother. She was a Firestarter, prayer warrior, and a true
friend of God. She had her faults, but her prayer life was a
wonderful testimony of her faith, and that is why I am honoring her
life by dedicating this book to her memory.

Table of Contents

Introduction:

In October 2015, I released my first prayer journal, Don't Stop Knocking, Don't Stop Seeking, Don't Stop Praying, Don't Stop Believing. I created the prayer journal because I needed a space to track my prayer requests, the scriptures I used to pray, the revelations I received, as well as the answers God provided, but unfortunately regular journals did not provide the space I needed. So, I decided to create what was missing, mostly for myself, but as I soon realized other people wanted this type of journal as well.

When I released Don't Stop Knocking, Don't Stop Seeking, Don't Stop Praying, Don't Stop Believing, I was shocked at the number of people who purchased the journal from all over the world and I knew that what I came up with was a God-given idea. The number of people looking to learn more about prayer journaling created an overflow of emotion in me that I can hardly describe.

While Don't Stop Knocking, Don't Stop Seeking, Don't Stop Praying, Don't Stop Believing has been available since October 2015, I still believe that it is a necessary resource for all believers who understand (or want to understand.) the power of prayer. In 2018, I held my first workshop on prayer journaling and again was amazed at how many people were interested in the subject of prayer journaling. People wanted to learn more, and I was excited to teach them what I knew, but one day as I was promoting the workshops I was presented with the challenge of creating a guide for people who are new to prayer and new to the faith. I honestly had not thought of creating a guideline or template before that challenge simply because I failed to see the need. But I thank God that He places people in our lives who ask tough questions.

This book is designed to guide anyone who desires to journal their prayers through the simple, yet essential process of prayer journaling. I pray that this guidance is what you need to help you effectively journal your prayers.

Prayer – The Great Exchange

Prayer is a communication with God and despite the many books on prayer; it does not require any specialized training. Prayer, in its most basic form, can be as simple as "Help Lord" or as long as a small book. Prayer is talking to God and hearing His reply, which often means waiting for His response.

When I gave my life to Christ, I was 13 years old. I grew up in church my entire life; in fact, I can remember sitting on the front pew with my paternal grandmother, Eula Fuller with my black Mary Janes and white stockings. God was an essential part of my family, and we believed in prayer. When one of us was sick or hurt, my Grandmom would always pull out her anointed oil pray for us. It did not matter who needed prayer or what the sickness or injury was, my Grandmother believed that God could heal. She would grab the oil, sit us down, put the oil on our forehead or when appropriate the affected body part and she would pray in faith believing that God would heal. My Grandmother was our families' example of prayer, and it was something that many of us have followed throughout our lives.

I will never forget being at my father's house one weekend, and while I was there, my sister Rhonda developed a problem with her legs. While I don't remember what the issue was, I remember standing around my Dad's bed watching him, and my stepmother prayed for Rhonda's legs to be healed. After they prayed, they took Rhonda to the doctor and not long after, Rhonda's legs healed completely. For my family, prayer was and is an essential tool, and it has become increasingly more important to me personally.

In the beginning, prayer between God and Adam was a conversation. God himself walked the earth with Adam and conversed with him, and Adam talked with God. God loved Adam and desired to be with him, and that's why He created Adam. He took Adam's every need into consideration, including his need for companionship and that is why God created Eve as Adam's mate. (reference Genesis 2:7-25). Just like He did with Adam and Eve, God desires to be with us and for us to be "naked and unashamed" before him. For Adam and Eve, "naked and unashamed" meant that they were literally naked and unashamed in the garden, but for us "naked and unashamed" means to be utterly transparent before God.

Being wholly transparent or naked and unashamed before God in prayer means to give everything to God in prayer. It means to hold nothing back from Him because He sees it all anyway. How do we know that? We know that because His Word tells us that He is omnipresent (present everywhere at the same time).

> *"Am I a God near at hand," says the Lord, "And, not a God afar off? Can anyone hide himself in secret places, So I shall not see him?" says the Lord; "Do I not fill heaven and earth?" says the Lord. ~ Jeremiah 23:23-24 NKJV*

> *The eyes of the Lord are in every place, keeping*

watch on the evil and the good. ~ Proverbs 15:3 NKJV

So, He sees all the good, all the bad, all the ugly anyway, and guess what He wants us to bring it all to Him.

When I created my prayer journal, I was finally beginning to understand some of the principles I am telling you now. I was on a prayer journey with God, and during my journey, my prayer life catapulted to a new level. I have always had a prayer life, but my prayer life now is at a greater degree and journaling my prayers helped me along my journey, so I want to teach you some of the principles I learned so that you too can take your prayer life to the next level. Remember, God is not far off from you, He wants to be close to you; intimate with you, and prayer is one of the ways He wants to do that.

The Journey of Prayer & Answers

Prayer for most people involves talking – lots of talking, but at some point, we must listen. As I stated in the previous chapter, prayer, in its purest form is a conversation between you and God. Conversation is the informal exchange of ideas by spoken words, and we know that in an exchange there is give and take so, our prayer time should always include space for God to speak.

God speaks in various ways, and it is not always audible. I know that there are some who, like me, hear God audibly, but I know that there are just as many that "hear" God in a change in their mood, their thoughts, or "hear" God through others. It is important not to place God in a box or limit God in your expectation of His answers, but trust that God can answer your prayer prayed in faith. I don't want you to get hung up on the "how" because honestly, that's God's job because He knows you better than YOU know yourself. He knows all about you, literally everything so He knows how to best communicate with you so that you hear Him, receive from Him and believe Him.

O Lord, you have examined me, and you know me. You alone know when I sit down and when I get up. You read my thoughts from far away. You watch me when I travel and when I rest. You are familiar with all my ways. Even before there is a [single] word on my tongue, you know all about it, Lord. You are all around me—in front of me and in back of me. You lay your hand on me. Such knowledge is beyond my grasp. It is so high I cannot reach it. Where can I go [to get away] from your Spirit? Where can I run [to get away] from you? If I go up to heaven, you are there. If I make my bed in hell, you are there. If I climb upward on the rays of the morning sun [or] land on the most distant shore of the sea where the sun sets, even there your hand would guide me and your right hand would hold on to me. If I say, "Let the darkness hide me and let the light around me turn into night," even the darkness is not too dark for you. Night is as bright as day. Darkness and light are the same [to you]. You alone created my inner being. You knitted me together inside my mother. I will give thanks to you because I have been so amazingly and miraculously made. Your works are miraculous, and my soul is fully aware of this. My bones were not hidden from you when I was being made in secret, when I was being skillfully woven in an underground workshop. Your eyes saw me when I was only a fetus. Every day [of my life] was recorded in your book before one of them had taken place. How precious are your thoughts concerning me, O God! How vast in number they are! If I try to count them, there would be more of them than there are grains of sand. When I wake up, I am still with you. ~ Psalm 139:1-18 GW

Now that you know that God knows you that intimately, you should know that He will make sure He responds to you in a way that works for you. This can be very different for everyone because we are all different, but our loving God knows all of us intimately and can respond to each of our individual needs.

When we come to God with problems, He listens to us, but not only does He hear us, he also wants to communicate a solution, a word or a revelation to help us. But often, we are so caught up in talking to God that we end our prayer time having done all the talking but have not stopped long enough to listen to what God might want to say. We forget to leave room in our prayer time for God to answer. I will be the first to admit to you, that I have spent countless hours in prayer talking my head off to God, but I never left space for the Lord to speak to me. The problem with that is God wants to communicate, but if I never give Him an opportunity to say anything I may end up missing my answer.

Now let me be clear, not every prayer you pray will get answered in your designated prayer time. Some answers come immediately, but some answers take time. The goal is to make room in your life so that you hear God when He answers. That means taking time to be quiet and listen; that means being open and available to God (naked and unashamed). We should live our lives so that we are always open to receive what God is saying. I am a firm believer that God is still speaking, but we, at times, are too busy to hear Him. The key is that we must make room for God to intervene in our lives. I found in my prayer journey that giving God space to answer in my prayer time also gave Him space to talk at other times in my life. In allowing God to speak in my prayer time, I allowed my life to be opened for God to begin to speak throughout my life causing a change in other areas that I may or may not have addressed in prayer. I became "naked and unashamed" before Him, and that is what God wants from us – total access to our lives.

How to Journal Your Prayers

Now that we have a better understanding of the importance of the great exchange of prayer let's talk about how to journal your prayers. When I first began my prayer journey, I was not journaling my prayers at all, then I started writing them down randomly here, there, and everywhere. I did not care what I wrote them down on, I just wrote down my prayers as I felt like it, but then I got frustrated with not being able to find the prayers I wrote down. I brought journals to keep my prayers in, but as a professed journal collector, I had prayers in all of them and not just prayers but regular journal entries too which became very confusing for me. So, I decided to create a journal that would help me keep track of my prayers because I was beginning to see a pattern of God answering and it was exhilarating for me, so I wanted to keep track of how He was answering me.

When I decided to create my own prayer journal, it was never really my intention to share it, but I felt led to release it. Feeling led is one of the ways God speaks to me; He gives me the motivation to do something (or not do something), and when I follow through He blesses me.

If you journal regularly, you already understand the concept of journaling or writing down events, feelings, times, seasons, etc. in one place that will later give you a way to reflect on what happened on a particular day or a specific season of your life (i.e. getting married, having a family, changing careers). Prayer

Journaling is like daily journaling in that you are keeping an account, but with prayer journaling we are keeping an account of our prayers.

There is no right or wrong way to journal your prayers, but there are benefits to prayer journaling, and we will talk about those shortly. Prayer Journaling is crucial for so many reasons, here are just a few reasons:

• Writing down your prayer requests provides focus when you are in your prayer time.

• Journaling your prayer requests provides clarity during prayer times.

• Journaling your prayer requests can serve as a reminder of what you need to pray about and keep you on track while praying.

• Prayer Journaling increases your faith when you see your prayers answered.

Practical Example:

Many times, people ask me why it so crucial to journal their prayers and I usually give this concrete example. How often have you gone to the store intending to get one thing, get to the store and get everything else but what you expected? I have. I can remember one case, in particular, I went to our local Wal-Mart to pick up some toilet paper because we had one roll left and I did not want us to run out. I walked into Wal-Mart, and I immediately got sidetracked at the home goods section. I got a cart because I knew that I wanted to pick up a few other things while I was at Wal-

Mart, but instead of going directly to the paper section, I walked around Super Wal-Mart picking up stuff as I came upon them. Now, if you have never been in a Super Wal-Mart, you know that it is a massive mix of Wal-Mart and Supermarket and it is the worst place to go when you want one thing because most people will ultimately leave with more than they intended.

When it was time to check out, I kept looking in my cart thinking "What I am forgetting?" I racked my brain trying to remember what I forgot, but it never came to me, so I checked out with what was in my cart and when I arrived home I remembered what I went to Wal-Mart for, toilet paper, but I did not pick it up, so I had to go back to Wal-Mart to get it. If I had written a list, I would not have forgotten the toilet paper or at the very least would've remembered it when I looked in my cart and checked what I had in the cart to what was on my list. How often has that happened to you? We love to think that we will remember everything, but the truth is that sometimes we do forget.

One of the other things I have learned since beginning my prayer journey is that the enemy loves to steal our thoughts when it comes to prayer and that is his nature. The Bible tells us, "The thief does not come except to steal, and to kill, and to destroy. I have come that they may have life and that they may have it more abundantly" – John 10:10 NKJV. The enemy does not just come to try to kill and destroy us. He also comes to steal from us, and that does not always mean our possessions, but it means he wants to steal anything God can use in us. In this case, it can be our memory to pray for something or for someone.

I do not take my prayer assignments lightly so for me, remembering is essential, and that is why I journal my prayers especially prayers that I pray for others, so I don't have to worry about not remembering those requests. Prayer Journaling ensures that I remember the prayer requests I have and those entrusted to my care. Prayer is important because I know that God answers faith-filled prayers, so I never want to miss an opportunity for God to get the glory by answering my prayers.

As important as it is to chronicle your prayers, it is just as essential to chronicle what God says to you in the way that you hear from him. We must understand that God is not obligated to repeat Himself, so it is up us to keep track of what God has spoken to us. That does not mean that God will not speak again, because He can and sometimes will, but it's best to catch what He's saying the first time, so we don't miss it. We never want to miss what God is saying or doing because we failed to listen and chronicle what He said. We also honor God when we write down what He says to us. I like to think of it as letting God know I am listening to Him and when I go back to read what He has said, it blesses me tremendously.

The next part of prayer journaling is my favorite part – it is journaling the answers God gives! I love it when God answers my prayers because that gives me something to talk about to everyone I know and even people I do not know. That prayer that God answered now becomes my testimony, and it excites me, and it excites others about what God can do for them. The fact of the matter is that despite what people say about Him, God does not have favorites and what He will do for me, He can do for you or anyone else.

> *If you go against the grain, you get splinters, regardless of which neighborhood you're from, what your parents taught you, what schools you attended. But if you embrace, the way God does things, there are wonderful payoffs, again without regard to where you are from or how you were brought up. Being a Jew won't give you an automatic stamp of approval. God pays no attention to what others say (or what you think) about you. He makes up his own mind. ~ Romans 2:9-11 MSG*

> *Come and hear, all who fear God [and worship Him with awe-inspired reverence and obedience.], and I will tell what He has done for me.~ Psalm 66:16 AMP*

Prayer Journaling Sections:

While I wrote this book as a companion guide to my prayer journal, Don't Stop Knocking, Don't Stop Seeking, Don't Stop Praying, Don't Stop Believing, you can use any journal to journal your prayers. I recommend Don't Stop Knocking, Don't Stop

Seeking, Don't Stop Praying, Don't Stop Believing because it contains all the sections you will need to journal your prayers successfully. There are four sections in Don't Stop Knocking, Don't Stop Seeking, Don't Stop Praying, Don't Stop Believing – prayer request, key scriptures, revelation, and answers. Each section is significant, but you may not use every section every time you journal your prayers, and that is normal. As I explain each section, you will understand why you may not use every section each time you journal your prayers.

Prayer Request:

The prayer request section is for all your prayer requests. You can choose to add as much or as little detail as you would like in this section. You can also add as many requests in this section as you deem necessary. As I said before there is no right or wrong way to journal your prayers, the important thing is to journal your prayers.

Key Scriptures:

The key scriptures section is to write down any scriptures you use in your prayer time. The Bible is God's Word, and ultimately we want to say what God says about everything. We also want to focus our prayers on what the Word of God has already said, not just on what we want to say. God is the final authority on all matters, and His Word is the ultimate Word on all matters great and small so praying His Word can catapult our prayer lives.

For example, when I pray for healing I use Isaiah 53:5 as my key scripture, *"But he was wounded for our transgressions, he was bruised for our iniquities: the chastisement of our peace was upon him; and with his stripes we are healed"* ~ Isaiah 53:5 KJV. If you come upon a situation where you are not sure what scripture to use, simply Google the area you want to pray about and the word "scriptures." You will get results that you can look at, meditate on and apply during your own prayer time.

Many have asked me how to incorporate scriptures in their prayer time, so I want to give an example of what this might look like using a prayer that I have prayed for someone recently diagnosed with an illness.

> ***Father, I thank you for your Word. I thank you for your power. I thank that you are God and above you, there is no one else. I come before you first asking you to forgive me of any sin that I have committed in word, thought or deed. Lord, forgive me for anything that I've done – knowingly or unknowingly – that would hinder my prayers this day. Lord, I thank for your forgiveness and I thank you that as your child I can come boldly to your throne and ask you for what I need because your word says that I can ask you anything in your name, yes, anything, and you will do it (John 14:13-14) so today Father, I come asking for healing for my sister. Lord, you are Jehovah Rapha***

(Exodus 15:26)– the God who heals. I believe that your Word is true and that you can heal. Lord, you know the diagnosis the doctors have given her, but Father I believe that you are greater than any diagnosis, disease, or infirmity. Lord, your report is greater and better than any report of the doctor so, Lord today I lift up my sister before you asking you Lord to heal her body completely and totally in Jesus' name. Father, let there be no residual pain or issue God. I pray for total and complete healing for her from the crown of her head to the very soles of her feet including her toes God. Heal her Lord! Lord, your Word says in Isaiah 53:5 that you were wounded for our transgressions, bruised for our iniquities, the chastisement of our peace was upon you; and with your stripes we are healed" and we believe your Word is true! Lord, because my sister has committed her life to you and said yes to you Jesus this is a promise for her just like it is for me so I pray that you would heal her as your word says. Lord, I don't care how you do it because I have learned that your ways are so much higher and better than mine so I choose not to put you in a box by telling you how to do it, I am merely asking you to heal her Father however you see fit. Lord, I thank you in advance for healing my sister so that

she will be able to live and testify about your goodness and healing power. I pray Father that you would also bless my sister with long life and length of days so that she can accomplish that which you have created her to do on the earth. Father, I thank you in advance for your healing, and I decree and declare that it is happening now in Jesus' name because of my faith and the faith of those who also believe for her healing. Lord, I thank you and praise you in Jesus' name, Amen.

I know that may seem long to some but as you can see I used several scriptures when I prayed this prayer not just one, but this was just an example, feel free to use as many scriptures as you think is necessary. I should also say that there are times when I do not use key scriptures in my prayer time, so I leave that section blank. Again, using the section is not required, but it can help you if you desire to pray God's word regarding a situation.

As I mentioned, I know this may be a long prayer to some, but I want to share something with you so that you are never discouraged. It is not the length of your prayer that matters; some people pray a lot longer than others, and some pray very short prayers. It is not the length of your prayers or how you sound praying that matters, it is your faith that makes the difference. So, no matter what the length of your prayers, have faith and believe the prayers that you pray.

Revelation:

We define revelations as an act of revealing or communicating divine truth; something that is revealed by God to humans. "An act of revealing to view or making known. Something that is revealed; especially an enlightening or astonishing disclosure." – Revelation - https://www.merriam-webster.com/dictionary/revelation.

In this section, you will want to write down anything that is revealed to you as you pray or after you've prayed. A revelation could be the same as your answer, or it could be very different. A revelation could be an insight into what you are praying about. It could be the knowledge that you did not have before that could change your prayer assignment. For example, I was praying and asking God for something, and when the opportunity came to get what I prayed for, I hesitated and could not understand why. When I prayed and asked why I hesitated, God revealed to me was that I was fearful about what I was asking for and I needed to deal with the fear before I could move forward. God already told me that I could have what I was asking for and I believed Him, but fear was keeping me away from securing what He said I could have. In this scenario, I had my answer, but the revelation I received that I was fearful was key because I would not have been able to obtain in fear. Fear was preventing me from securing the thing which God said I could have, and since He's never one to go against our will, He had to reveal to me the fear in my heart, so I could address that and get my answer.

This section is not necessary as you may not receive a revelation about each prayer request, but as with the other sections it is there if you need it.

Answers:

The answers section is my favorite section because this is where you get to share how God answered your prayers. Like the other sections, it is not necessary, but I strongly recommend that you use it. In fact, if you are going journal your prayers, I highly recommend that you journal God's answers to you, not just to encourage others but to encourage yourself. I cannot tell you how many times I have gone over all the ways that God has answered my prayers for finances, resources, and even vacations. Whatever God has done for me, He can do for you, but you must have the faith to believe that He can and will. In the next chapter, I want to share with you one of my testimonies so you can see how God answered my prayer. I can tell you that I was amazed when He did it, but because He answered my prayer a year later, had I not journaled the prayer request I would not have remembered even praying for what He provided.

A Chronicle of Answers

One of the most beautiful things about writing down my prayers has been seeing the hand of God in my life. Every time I go back and read through my prayers, I see His hand on my life through answered prayers, revelations, Godly wisdom, and more. It is so precious when I go back and read what God himself said about me or about an issue that I was facing; just thinking about it makes me emotional. The God who made the world; the God who created every living thing is talking to me about me and not just any old thing, He's talking good stuff about what He wants to do for me; where He's taking me and even how much He loves me – it is a fantastic experience.

When I began journaling my prayers, I didn't always capture what He told me or the answers to my prayers, but once I did, I started to see His love for me in a new way. My intimacy with God grew because I heard Him more and the more I listened, the more He spoke, to the point that I just wanted to sit and listen to Him all the time. I would at times feel like a little girl just waiting for everyone else to go away so I could talk to Him and He could speak to me. That is a far cry from where I was a few years ago, but when God starts to change you, and you allow Him, it's a fantastic experience. Now, that is not to say that my life is without issue or flaw because I am not perfect, but it does mean that God hears me, and I hear Him.

Journaling the answers to your prayers provides testimony

to you and others. It is also a great reminder of God's love when you are overwhelmed by what's happening around you currently. Looking back at what God has already done or said reminds you that if God did it before, He could do it again. Going over my answered prayers came in handy for me when I was having a rough time a couple of years ago. As I read through my prayer journal from back in August 2014, I came across a testimony. Back in 2014, I had asked God to send me on vacation because I was tired. I told God I needed him to send me away and I needed him to pay for it because I was tired. Life went on, and over the next year, I forgot about that prayer, but God did not forget about me or the request, and in August of 2015, He set me up to go on that vacation I prayed about a year earlier.

In late July 2015, I received an email from a very prominent computer company inviting me to Hollywood, Florida for an exclusive tech show. Included in the email was a link to the hotel where the event would take place, and the email stated the accommodations and meals were complimentary, but I had to pay for my flight and transportation to and from the hotel. I should say that as an IT Professional by trade, I get these types of emails all the time, and I had a practice of deleting them quickly, but for some reason this one was different. When I clicked on the hotel link, I knew I needed to be there, and I registered right away before I even discussed it with my manager. Once I registered, I sent my manager an email asking her if I could use training time to go to Florida and training funds to pay for the flight, but she did not respond immediately, so I waited for her response.

A few days later, a representative from the computer company called me to see if I still wanted to attend. I told him that I wanted to participate, but I did not receive a confirmation that my firm was willing to pay for the flight or allow me to use training time. When he heard that he said, "so all you need is the flight? I think we can cover that." Needless to say, I was stunned. He told me he would check with his manager to be sure and get back to me later that day with an answer. Later that night, my former Bishop prayed with me and we believed together in faith that the company would pay for my flight to Florida and before I arrived home that night, there was an email in my inbox stating that the computer company was paying for the flight and round-trip ground transportation. Again, I was amazed, excited, and elated!

I met with my manager the next day, and she informed that I would need to use my vacation days to attend the meeting, which was fine with me. The next few days were a buzz getting myself together to go away and even though it was just for a few days, it was the break I needed. Before leaving for Florida, the company sent me my itinerary via email, and I found out that a chauffeured car would be picking me up from the airport. As many times as I saw the chauffeured vehicles pick up people in front of my law firm, or on TV, I personally never had the experience yet it was something I always wanted, and it was about to happen.

When I left Connecticut, I knew that I would be coming back a different person because I was about to experience something I never had before and I am a firm believer that when I encounter something great I've never had before, it is God showing me glimpses of my future so that I can run after it. When I boarded the first flight, it was full, so I could not sit near the window, so I read my book. The second leg of my trip, the plane was nearly empty, so I sat next to a window and looked out on the sky. It was nighttime at that point, and we were flying right into a storm, but for some reason, I was not afraid. I could see the lighting and hear the thunder below us as we flew over the storm. At one point, we started to fly up and over the storm in such a way that I could look down and see lightning and what looked like the hand of God over that region. It was almost like God was protecting that land. I don't know where we were at the time, but I was amazed at the beauty of the storm.

When I arrived in Florida, just as the company told me, a driver was waiting for me at the airport to take me to the hotel in a black Mercedes Benz SUV. As the driver pulled up to the hotel, I was in awe, even at night the hotel was immaculate. When I walked into the hotel, I was stunned by the majesty of the lobby and entrance; it was breathtaking. I had stayed in hotels before, but this place was amazing. There were palm trees in the lobby, and the décor was gorgeous.

After I checked in, I headed straight up to my room and again I was at a loss for words. My room had a wraparound balcony with magnificent views of both the intercostal waters and the ocean. The room was appointed with everything I needed for my stay. There were even Starbucks coffee pods right there in the room. At the time, Starbucks was my favorite coffee, and that little detail meant so much to me. God took care of every single aspect and desire I had for a vacation, and I was so thankful because this was everything I needed and so much more. I was also grateful because just as I prayed this beautiful vacation was something I did not have to pay for; just like I prayed the year before, I was on vacation, and I did not have to pay for anything.

The next day, the company had a catered breakfast waiting for us. They also had a catered lunch prepared, and in between meals we were able to see some of their new technology before anyone else. For me, this was the best vacation I had ever been on with all my favorite things – new technology, beautiful scenery, beautiful beaches, tranquil surroundings, and Starbucks coffee. I couldn't have asked for a better vacation. The company spared no expense for my hotel room, and meals and they catered to my every need. The company even paid for us to take a water taxi tour of the intercostal waters before our catered dinner. Everything I wanted and needed was taken care of and I was speechless. I had a fantastic time, and honestly, I could not have planned the vacation any better if I had tried. God knew what He was doing. The thing that amazes me still is that I used to get emails like that all the time, but this one was tailor-made for me. No one else in my company received the email, and no one else in my state received the email. In fact, when a representative contacted me about the itinerary, she told me I was coming the furthest away, and they usually did not pick people from such a far distance. I knew that it was not their choice really, it was God answering my prayer because He knows me so well.

Looking back at my journal entry asking the Lord to send me on vacation, I can tell you that only God could've orchestrated something so magnificent and something so tailor-made for me. It was amazing and because I wrote down that prayer I was also able to see how God answered me even though it was a year later. I had a record of asking and a record of God answering. But, had I not written down that prayer in 2014, I would not have been able to track back how God responded because I honestly did not remember crying out in prayer asking for God to send me on vacation.

So, when I find myself melancholy, I can look back at this testimony and receive a boost that God hears and answers prayer. The answers that I chronicled also serve a fantastic testimony that I can share with others just as I shared with you. There are so many other instances that I could relay, but I believe I have made my point – writing down your prayers provides a fantastic testimony for you about God's amazing love. (If you'd like to see some of the photos from the trip, I've included some of the pictures at the end of this book).

If you need a place to write down your requests, you can purchase a copy of *Don't Stop Knocking, Don't Stop Seeking, Don't Stop Praying, Don't Stop Believing* from my website, ThoughtsofaThankfulHeart.com or wherever books are sold.

I pray that this has been a blessing to you; I pray that as you journal your prayers, revelations, and answers, you will find all the treasures God has for you.

A Visual Display of Answered Prayer

My chauffeured car from the airport.

The view of my hotel from the intercostal water taxi.

Elevator selfie!

The daytime view from my hotel balcony

The hotel lobby.

The hotel lobby

Daytime views from the balcony

View from the intercostal water taxi.

View from the intercoastal water taxi

The evening view from my hotel balcony

The evening view from the other side of my hotel balcony.

ABOUT THE AUTHOR

Liela Marie Fuller is an Author, Speaker, and Entrepreneur. Liela is a transparent author – unashamed to put her life in print. In Life's Reflection, her first poetry book, she invited us deep into her world, gripping us with passionate pieces like "Black Rose," "Is Love What You Call It," and "Addicted." Liela's transparency in the face of trials attracted the attention of many readers and has generated a strong following. In 2015, Liela released her second book, Love Letters of a Worshipper: Poetry, Prose and Prayers and once again Liela's transparency was evident as she let readers in on one of the most intimate relationships in her life – her relationship with God. Liela wowed readers with beautiful ballads like "Resolute" and "God Can Have Everything I Have." Through her transparency, Liela strives to share with and strengthen the resolve and hope of those who read her work. Liela has created several journals including- Don't Stop Knocking, Don't Stop Seeking, Don't Stop Praying, Don't Stop Believing! A Prayer Journal – A Dream Journal and God's Daily Provision, and Speak Lord – A Word Journal.

Liela is originally from Camden, NJ, she is the owner of Jadora's Child Publishing and Heavenly Help Computer Solutions.

You can connect with Liela on Facebook, Twitter, Instagram, and Periscope. To book Liela as a speaker for your event, email MerkMediaCT@gmail.com.

.

Made in the USA
Middletown, DE
16 June 2021